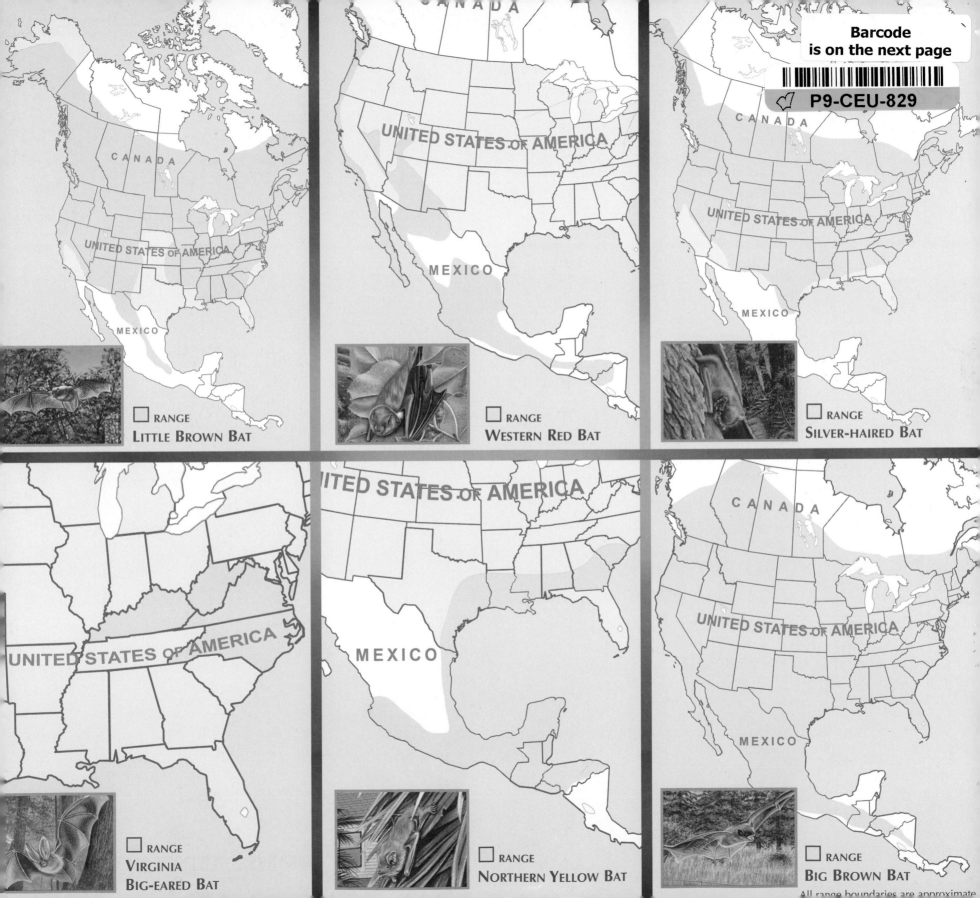

☐ RANGE
LITTLE BROWN BAT

☐ RANGE
WESTERN RED BAT

☐ RANGE
SILVER-HAIRED BAT

☐ RANGE
VIRGINIA
BIG-EARED BAT

☐ RANGE
NORTHERN YELLOW BAT

☐ RANGE
BIG BROWN BAT

All range boundaries are approximate

A PLACE FOR
BATS

For Caroline Grace
—*M. S.*

For Patrycja Bond with gratitude
—*H. B.*

Ω

Published by
PEACHTREE PUBLISHERS
1700 Chattahoochee Avenue
Atlanta, Georgia 30318-2112

www.peachtree-online.com

Text © 2012 by Melissa Stewart
Illustrations © 2012 by Higgins Bond

Book design by Loraine M. Joyner
Composition by Maureen Withee
Illustrations created in acrylic on cold press illustration board.
Title typeset in Hardlyworthit; main text typeset in Monotype's Century Schoolbook with Optima initial capitals. Sidebars typeset in Optima.

Printed and manufactured by Imago in October 2011 in Singapore
10 9 8 7 6 5 4 3 2 1
First Edition

Library of Congress Cataloging-in-Publication Data
Stewart, Melissa.
 A place for bats / written by Melissa Stewart ; illustrated by Higgins Bond. -- 1st ed.
    p. cm.
ISBN 13: 978-1-56145-624-6 / ISBN 10: 1-56145-624-1
 1. Bats--Juvenile literature. I. Bond, Higgins, ill. II. Title.
 QL737.C5S7447 2012
 599.4--dc23
                    2011020468

A PLACE FOR
BATS

Written by
Melissa Stewart

Illustrated by
Higgins Bond

PEACHTREE
ATLANTA

Bats make our world a better place. But sometimes people do things that make it hard for them to live and grow.

If we work together to help these winged creatures of the night, there will always be a place for bats.

MEXICAN FREE-TAILED BAT

ON THE WING

The tough, leathery skin that covers a bat's wings stretches between its long, thin finger bones. By moving its fingers ever so slightly, the flying fur ball can change its direction at lightning speed. By zigzagging, dipping, and diving, a bat can easily catch an insect in midair with its back feet. Then the hungry hunter pops the prey into its mouth.

For bats to survive, they need to stay safe and healthy. Many bats are killed by people who think bats are dangerous.

INDIANA BAT

In the 1800s, millions and millions of Indiana bats spent the winter in caves in Kentucky, Missouri, and Indiana. People snuck into some of the caves and killed bats one by one. People set fires inside other caves, so the bats would burn. By the 1960s, almost all the bats were gone. Today, groups like Bat Conservation International are letting people know that bats are an important part of our world. Hopefully, educating people will help save Indiana bats.

But bats can't hurt us, and they devour pesky insects all night long.
When people learn the truth about these little nighttime hunters,
bats can live and grow.

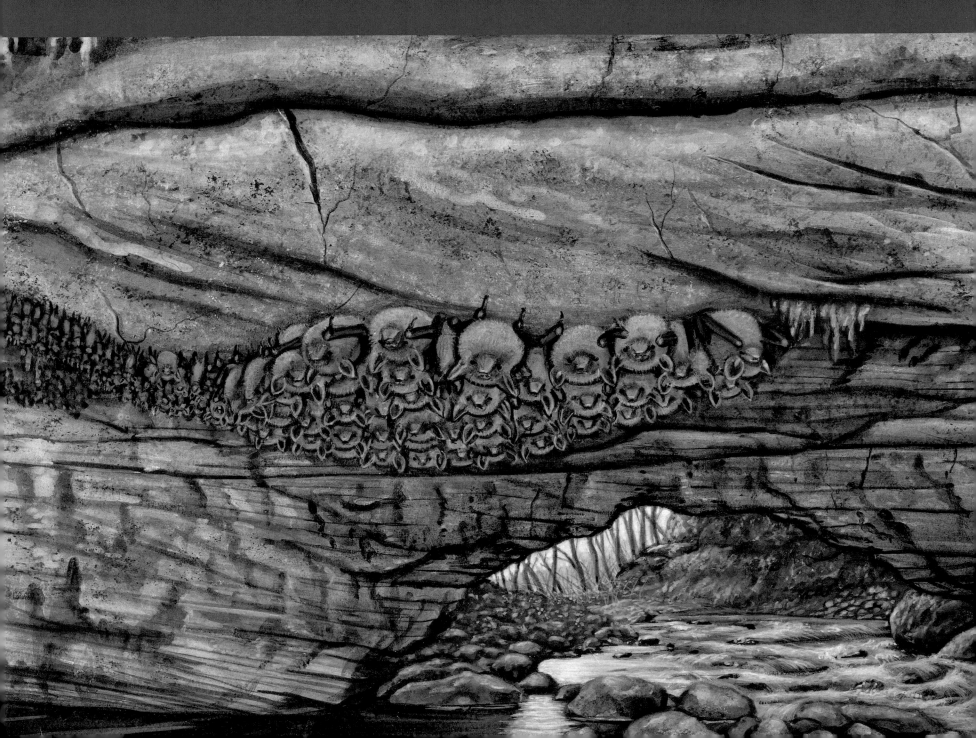

Some bats die when they fly too close to the wind turbines people use to make electricity.

HOARY BAT

In 2008, scientists discovered that when a hoary bat flies through the low-pressure area around a wind turbine's blades, the air inside its lungs suddenly expands. Blood vessels around the lungs burst, and the bat dies. Once scientists understood the problem, they figured out how to solve it. Bats are most active on calm nights, when wind turbines don't produce much power. If power companies turn off their turbines when the wind isn't blowing, they can save hoary bats and still produce plenty of electricity.

When people turn off wind turbines on calm nights,
bats can live and grow.

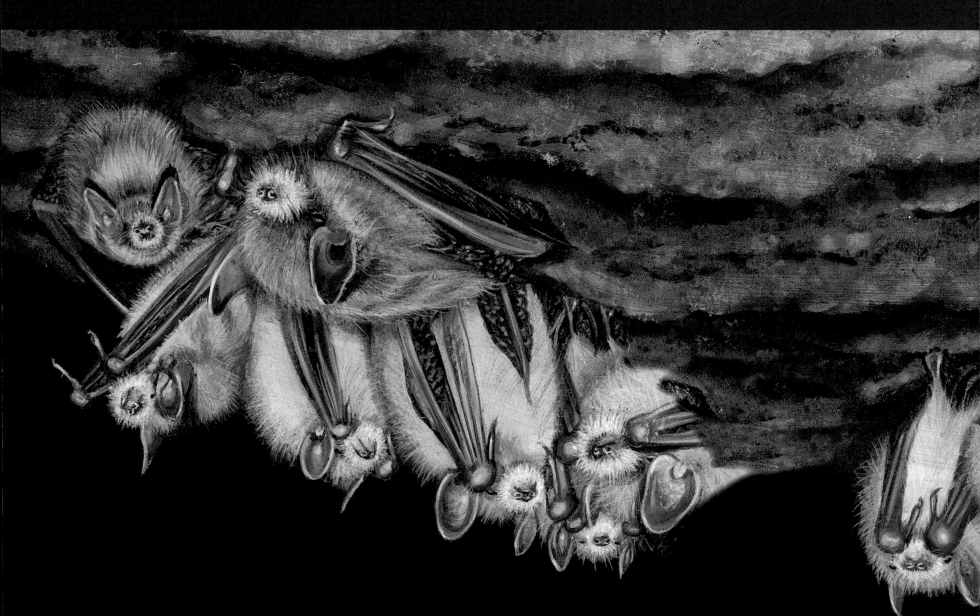

Thousands of bats are dying of a terrible disease called white nose syndrome. Some scientists think it may be caused by poisons used to kill insects.

When people stop spraying these dangerous chemicals, bats can live and grow.

EASTERN PIPISTRELLE

Since 2006, white nose syndrome has killed millions of bats, but scientists don't know why. Some researchers think that poisons sprayed to kill insects may be making eastern pipistrelles and other bats weak, so their bodies can't fight off a fungus that infects the bats' noses, ears, and wings. The poison may also wake bats out of hibernation too early. Since bats can't find insects to eat at that time of year, they starve to death. Scientists are looking for ways to treat white nose syndrome and help the bats.

Some bats spend their days sleeping in backyard trees.
If a hungry housecat spots these bats, it will attack.

EVENING BAT

At one time, evening
bats slept safely in deep,
dark forests. But as woodlands disappear, more and
more evening bats spend
their days in backyard trees.
Neighborhood noises can make
it hard for bats to sense dangers
like a prowling cat—until it's
too late. Keeping pet cats
indoors can save bats, birds,
and other small creatures
that visit our backyards.

When people keep their pet cats indoors,
bats can live and grow.

Bats also need safe places to raise their young. Some bat pups grow up inside caves.

When workers build gates to keep out curious explorers,
bats can live and grow.

GRAY BAT

Each summer, female gray
bats gather together and raise their
young inside caves. If people disturb
the bats, the mothers may fly away
and not return. Without mother's milk,
the pups starve to death. To protect gray
bats, workers are now building bat-
friendly gates that keep people out
of some caves.

Other mother bats raise their pups in small, hidden places.

LITTLE BROWN BAT

In the past, little brown bats raised their young under the peeling bark of dead trees. But then people began cutting down the dead trees on their land. Luckily, some people noticed the problem and started building bat boxes. Today you can see these boxes in backyards and wooded areas all over North America.

When people build bat boxes that are the right size and shape,
bats can live and grow.

Bats have trouble surviving when their home habitats are destroyed. Some bats can only live in open woodlands with rivers or streams nearby.

WESTERN RED BAT

Rich soil and warm temperatures make California's Central Valley perfect for growing crops. Because the area doesn't receive much rain, the best farmland is close to rivers. Over time, most of the woodlands where western red bats used to live have been turned into farms. But now people in Yolo and Kern Counties are working hard to protect land that has everything the bats need to survive.

When people set aside some of these natural areas,
bats can live and grow.

Other bats can only survive in thick forests with lots of large, old trees.

When people protect the land and the trees,
bats can live and grow.

SILVER-HAIRED BAT

For many years, forest rangers
in the western United States
cut down dead trees to help
protect old-growth forests from
wildfires. Scientists discovered
that silver-haired bats like to
roost under the loose bark on
dead trees, and without the
trees the bats had fewer places
to rest. Today, forest rangers let
many of the dead trees stand
so they can provide shelter for
bats and other forest creatures.

S̲ome bats eat just a few kinds of insects. And those insects depend on plants that only grow in hardwood forests.

VIRGINIA BIG-EARED BAT

Many bats eat lots of different insects, but not Virginia big-eared bats. Most of the time, they eat moths. And those moths feed on just two kinds of plants—wild grapevines and sourwood shrubs. When people build houses and shopping malls on the land where these plants grow, both the moths and the bats starve. In 2005, the Virginia big-eared bat became the official state bat of Virginia. Now people in that state are making efforts to save these bats and the forests where they hunt.

When people protect the forests where these plants live,
bats can live and grow.

Some bats spend their days sleeping in palm trees. They stay safe from enemies by hiding under dead, leaf-like fronds.

When people leave the old, drooping fronds on the trees in their yards,
bats can live and grow.

NORTHERN YELLOW BAT

Many people do not like
the way dead, brown fronds
look hanging from palm trees.
They trim the fronds so the trees
will look neat and tidy. But recently,
people in South Texas have realized
that northern yellow bats roost
under the fronds. So now some
area residents are leaving dead
fronds on their trees so the bats
have a safe place to sleep.

Thousands of bats can die when people block the openings of old, abandoned mines.

BIG BROWN BAT

Open mine shafts can be dangerous, so landowners often fill them in. But if there are bats inside, they will be buried alive. Just before Millie Hill Mine in Iron Mountain, Michigan, was supposed to be closed, scientists found millions of big brown bats inside. Instead of blocking the shaft, workers built a steel cage around the opening. Now bats can easily fly in and out, but no one will fall into the mine.

When people check old mines before filling them with rocks and dirt, bats can live and grow.

When too many bats die, other living things may also have trouble surviving.

PLANTS NEED BATS

In warm parts of the world, some bats sip sugary nectar from flowers. As they drink, the bats spread pollen from one flower to another. The plants use material in the pollen to make fruit with new seeds inside.

Other bats eat fruit. When the bats release their wastes, seeds land on the ground. If the soil is rich and moist, the seeds will grow into new plants. Bananas, peaches, avocados, dates, figs, and mangoes all depend on bats to spread their pollen and to carry their seeds to new places.

That's why it's so important to protect bats and the places where they live.

OTHER ANIMALS NEED BATS

Bats are an important part of the food chain. Hungry snakes, raccoons, opossums, skunks, and weasels sometimes prey on bats sleeping in trees. Hawks and owls can catch bats as they fly through the air. If too many bats disappear, their predators will have to work harder to find food.

LESSER LONG-NOSED BAT

Bats have lived on Earth for more than 50 million years.

Sometimes people do things that can harm bats. But there are many ways you can help these special creatures live far into the future.

HOW WE CAN HELP BATS

❖ Put up a bat house in the backyard.

❖ Start a wildlife garden with plants that attract moths and other nighttime insects for bats to eat.

❖ Don't spray chemicals that could harm bats.

❖ Don't enter caves if you think there might be bats inside.

❖ Join a group of people working to protect bats in your area.

❖ Sponsor a bat through an adopt-a-bat program.

FASCINATING BAT FACTS

Forty-five kinds of bats live in North America. Seven of them are on the endangered species list—gray bats, Indiana bats, Ozark bats, big-eared bats, Virginia big-eared bats, lesser long-nosed bats, Mexican long-nosed bats, and Hawaiian hoary bats.

No one knows exactly how many kinds of bats live on Earth. So far, scientists have discovered more than 1,100 different species.

The Kitti's hog-nosed bat is the smallest bat on Earth. It's about the size of a bumblebee. The flying fox is the world's largest bat. It's as long as two loaves of bread placed end to end, and its wings can stretch five feet.

Almost all of the bats in North America and 70 percent of bats worldwide eat insects. But some bats eat fruit, nectar, fish, frogs, lizards, and birds.

Blood-sucking vampire bats in Central and South America usually feed on chickens, turkeys, ducks, and geese. Sometimes they drink blood from pigs, cattle, and horses.

Bats are the only mammals that can fly. The big brown bat is the world's fastest bat. It can cruise through the air at forty miles per hour.

Bats can live up to twenty years. Most female bats have one pup each year, but western red bats can have up to four babies at once.

Acknowledgments

The Smithsonian National Museum of Natural History provided range maps and habitat data for most of the bats discussed in this book.

Selected Bibliography

BOOKS AND ARTICLES

Davies, Nicola. *Bat Loves the Night*. Cambridge, MA: Candlewick, 2004.*

Earle, Ann. *Zipping, Zapping, Zooming Bats*. New York: HarperCollins, 1995.*

Markle, Sandra. *Little Lost Bat*. Watertown, MA: Charlesbridge, 2009.*

Markle, Sandra. *Outside and Inside Bats*. New York: Walker & Company, 2004.*

"Scientists Say Bat Disease Likely to Spread." *All Things Considered*. National Public Radio, August 19, 2009, 20:00–21:00 P.M.

Stewart, Melissa. *How Do Bats Fly in the Dark?* Tarrytown, NY: Benchmark Books, 2009.*

Toops, Connie. "Going to Bat for Bats." *National Parks*. Jan–Feb 2001: pp. 28–31.

Tuttle, Merlin D. *America's Neighborhood Bats*. Austin, TX: University of Texas Press, 2005.

Tuttle, Merlin D. *The Bat House Builder's Handbook*, Completely Revised and Updated. Austin, TX: Bat Conservation International, 2005.

Williams, Kim, Rob Mies, and Donald and Lillian Stokes. *Stokes Beginner's Guide to Bats*. New York: Little, Brown & Company, 2002.*

WEBSITES

Bat Conservation International. URL at http://www.batcon.org/

Defenders of Wildlife: Bats. URL at http://www.defenders.org/wildlife_and_habitat/wildlife/bats.php#*

*Recommended resources for young explorers

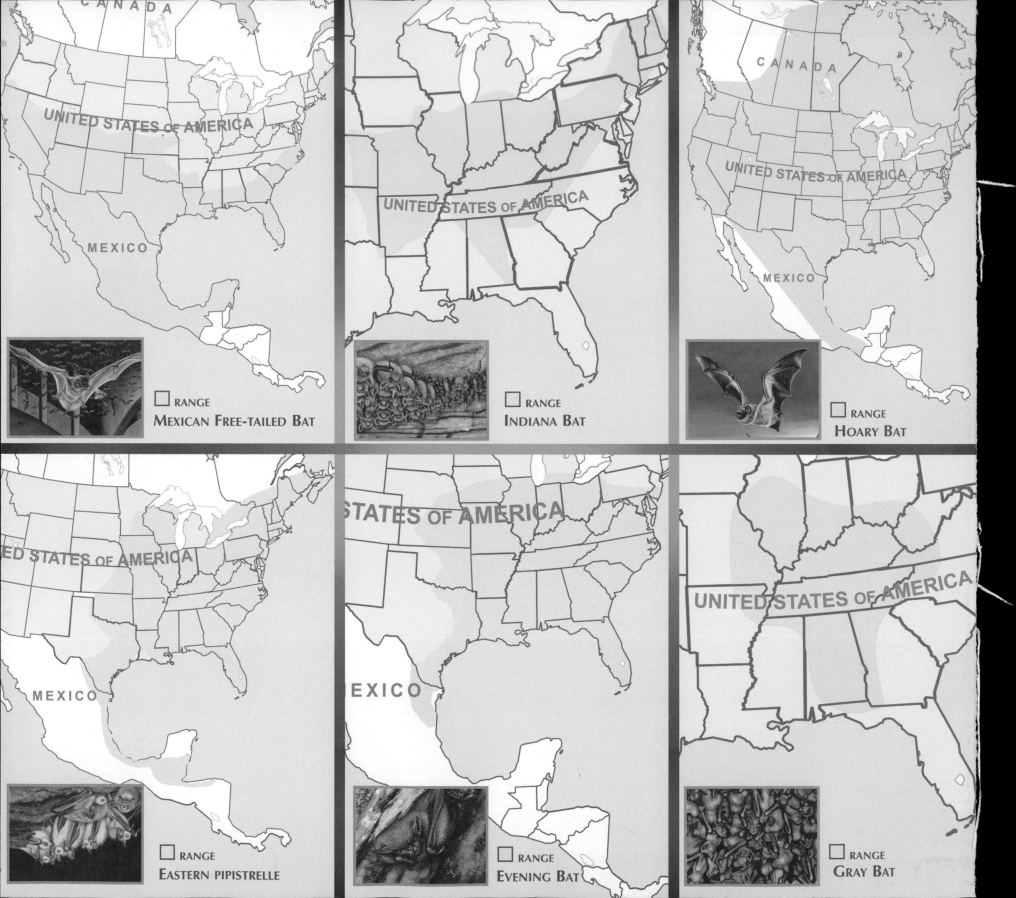

☐ RANGE
MEXICAN FREE-TAILED BAT

☐ RANGE
INDIANA BAT

☐ RANGE
HOARY BAT

☐ RANGE
EASTERN PIPISTRELLE

☐ RANGE
EVENING BAT

☐ RANGE
GRAY BAT